I0842477

COMET
MERCURY
SUN
MARS
VENUS
SATURN
JUPITER
NEPTUNE
URANUS

MERCURY
SUN

VENUS

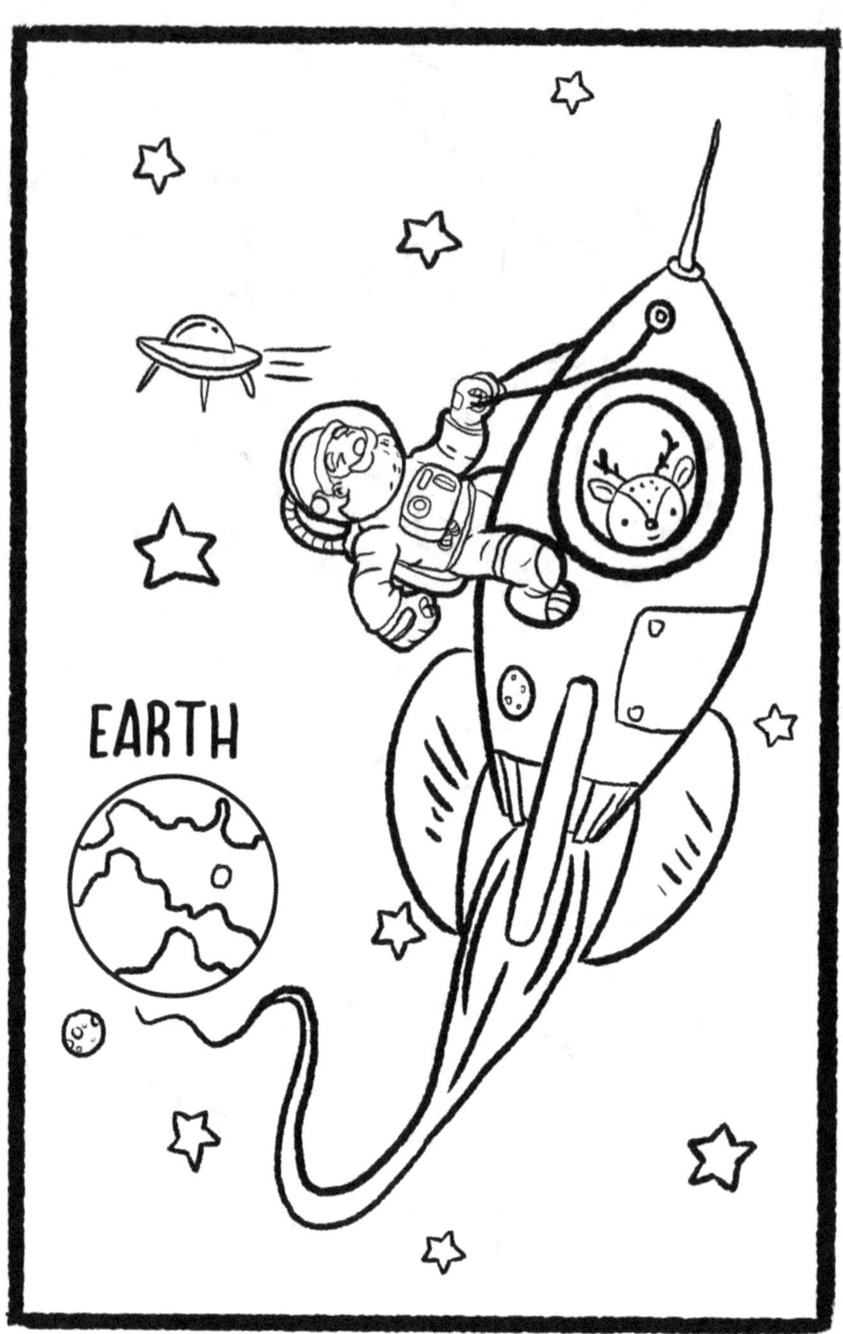

EARTH

HO! HO! HO!
MOON

MARS

MERRY CHRISTMAS
JUPITER

SATURN

URANUS

NEPTUNE

MERCURY

MARS

MERRY CHRISTMAS
OHO! HO! HO!
VENUS

JUPITER
HO! HO!
SATURN

HAPPY HOLIDAYS

MERRY
christmas

cosmic
christmas

SPACE
CHRISTMAS

MERRY
CRHISTMAS

HAPPY HOLIDAYS

MERRY CHRISTMAS!

BWOOP!
CHRISTMAS

www.ingramcontent.com/pod-product-compliance
Lightning Source LLC
Chambersburg PA
CBHW061541250726
48657CB00006B/2276